PENDULUM · GALLERY · PRESS ·
THE NEW SEX DIET!

BY TONI GOFFE

"ARE WE HAVING FUN YET?"

"FUN!? I THOUGHT THIS WAS A DIET BOOK"

First published in Great Britain by
Pendulum Gallery Press
56 Ackender Road, Alton, Hants GU34 1JS

© TONI GOFFE 1988

THE NEW SEX DIET
ISBN 0-948912-04-9

REPRINTED 1989, 1990

All rights reserved. No part of this publication may be reproduced or transmitted in any form or by any means, electronic or mechanical, including photocopying, recording, or any information storage and retrieval system, or for a source of ideas without permission in writing from the publisher

PRINTED IN GREAT BRITAIN BY
UNWIN BROTHERS LTD, OLD WOKING, SURREY

IS IT POSSIBLE TO LOSE WEIGHT DURING SEX?
SURE
WELL HOW MUCH?
THIS DEPENDS ON HOW MUCH PHYSICAL EFFORT YOU PUT INTO IT SO, STOP TALKING AND GET ON WITH IT!
PHYSICAL EFFORT BURNS CALORIES
FUR TOO!

EXAMPLE:

THIS COUPLE, DURING ONE HOUR OF SEX, LOST ONLY 2 CALORIES (THAT'S ONE EACH) AND THAT WAS JUST GETTING UNDRESSED!...

THE STUDY OF WEIGHT LOSS DURING SEX BECAME AN INDIVIDUAL PURSUIT...

THE STUDY OF WEIGHT LOSS DURING SEX FADED INTO OBSCURITY...

OR CHECK YOUR WEIGHT YOURSELF...

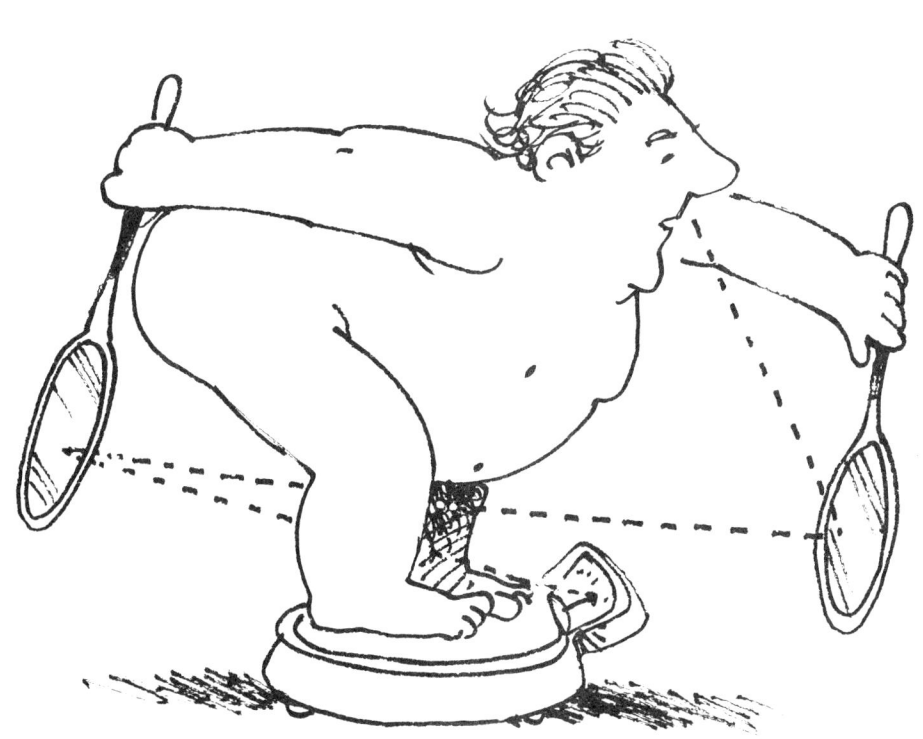

ONCE YOU'RE SURE YOU ARE OVERWEIGHT FIND OUT WHAT WEIGHT YOU SHOULD BE. BY LOOKING AT THIS CHART...

14 to 30 lbs.	3 ft.
31 to 42 lbs.	3 ft. 3 in.
43 to 54 lbs.	4 ft. ½ in.
55 to 65 lbs.	4 ft. 4 in.
66 to 77 lbs.	4 ft. 7 in.
78 to 90 lbs.	5 ft.
91 to 100 lbs.	5 ft. 3 in.
101 to 110 lbs.	5 ft. 5 in.
111 to 122 lbs.	5 ft. 7 in.
123 to 135 lbs.	5 ft. 9 in.
136 to 147 lbs.	5 ft. 11 in.
148 to 160 lbs.	6 ft. ¼ in.
161 to 172 lbs.	6 ft. 2 in.
173 to 185 lbs.	6 ft. 4 in.
186 to 200 lbs.	6 ft. 5 in.
201 to 212 lbs.	6 ft. 7 in.
213 to 225 lbs.	6 ft. 10 in.
226 to 240 lbs.	7 ft. 2 in.
241 to 255 lbs.	7 ft. 7 in.
256 to 270 lbs.	8 ft.

YOU'RE EITHER TOO HEAVY...

AS IT HAS BEEN PROVED, CHANGING YOUR HEIGHT IS BOTH PAINFUL...

SO YOU'RE STUCK WITH CHANGING YOUR WEIGHT...

NONE OF THESE DIETS WORK!

WITH THE EXCEPTION OF THE SURGICAL DIET!
THERE IS A CERTAIN AMOUNT OF WEIGHT LOSS.
ONCE THE PATIENT IS CAUGHT, TIED DOWN AND WORKED UPON...

IT IS NOT A POPULAR DIET...

THE ONE THING ABOUT **THE NEW SEX DIET**, IS THAT IT WORKS! THAT'S, OF COURSE, IF YOU KEEP "DOING IT!"
THERE ARE 3,500 CALORIES TO THE POUND, SO, IF YOU WANT LOSE WEIGHT YOU JUST HAVE TO KEEP DOING IT AND DOING IT AND DOING IT AND DOING IT AND DOING IT AND DOING IT AND DOING IT AND DOING IT...

NOW, ARE YOU FIT ENOUGH TO START!!?
IF YOU'RE NOT SURE, LOOK OUT FOR THESE SIGNS OF BEING UNFIT FOR THE NEW SEXDIET!

YOU'RE UNFIT WHEN YOU STOP TAKING THE DOG FOR A WALK...

YOU'RE UNFIT WHEN YOU GO TO BED WITH OTHER THINGS ON YOUR MIND THAN SEX!

YOU'RE UNFIT WHEN EATING BECOMES MORE IMPORTANT THAN SEX!

TO GET THE BEST RESULTS FROM THIS DIET, YOU NEED STAMINA. THE LONGER YOU INDULGE IN SEXUAL ACTIVITY THE MORE CALORIES YOU BURN OFF AND THEREFORE MORE WEIGHT YOU LOSE, SO....
GET YOURSELF **FIT** BEFORE YOU BEGIN THE DIET....

THE KEEP FIT PROGRAMME:

FIRST, THE PRESS-UP...

JOGGING CAN BE A LONELY PASTIME.

GET SOME FRIENDS TO ENCOURAGE YOU!...

SIT-UPS: SLIP YOUR FEET UNDER SOMETHING TO GIVE YOU SOME PURCHASE AND SIT UP...

YOGA: THE PLOUGH:

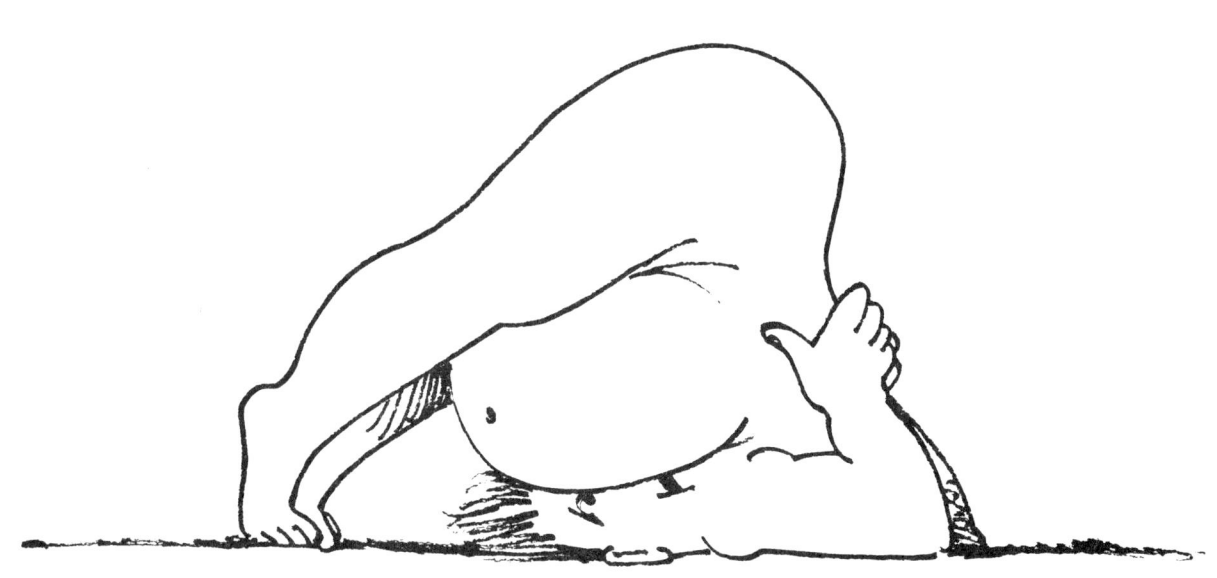

ONLY ATTEMPT THIS POSE IF YOU CAN BREATHE DURING IT!

ARE YOU FIT YET?

WELL. IF NOT. DON'T WORRY ABOUT IT! LET'S GET ON ...

...TO THE GOOD STUFF...

.... AND I MEAN ....

SEX WITH ONESELF:

IS'NT ALL FUN. BUT YOU DO MEET A BETTER CLASS OF PERSON.

THE RECORD OF WEIGHT LOSS DURING SEX WITH ONESELF...

.....IS DISMAL TO SAY THE LEAST...

.... SO...

WHILE REACHING FOR THE INSTRUCTIONS...

DON'T LET GO!!

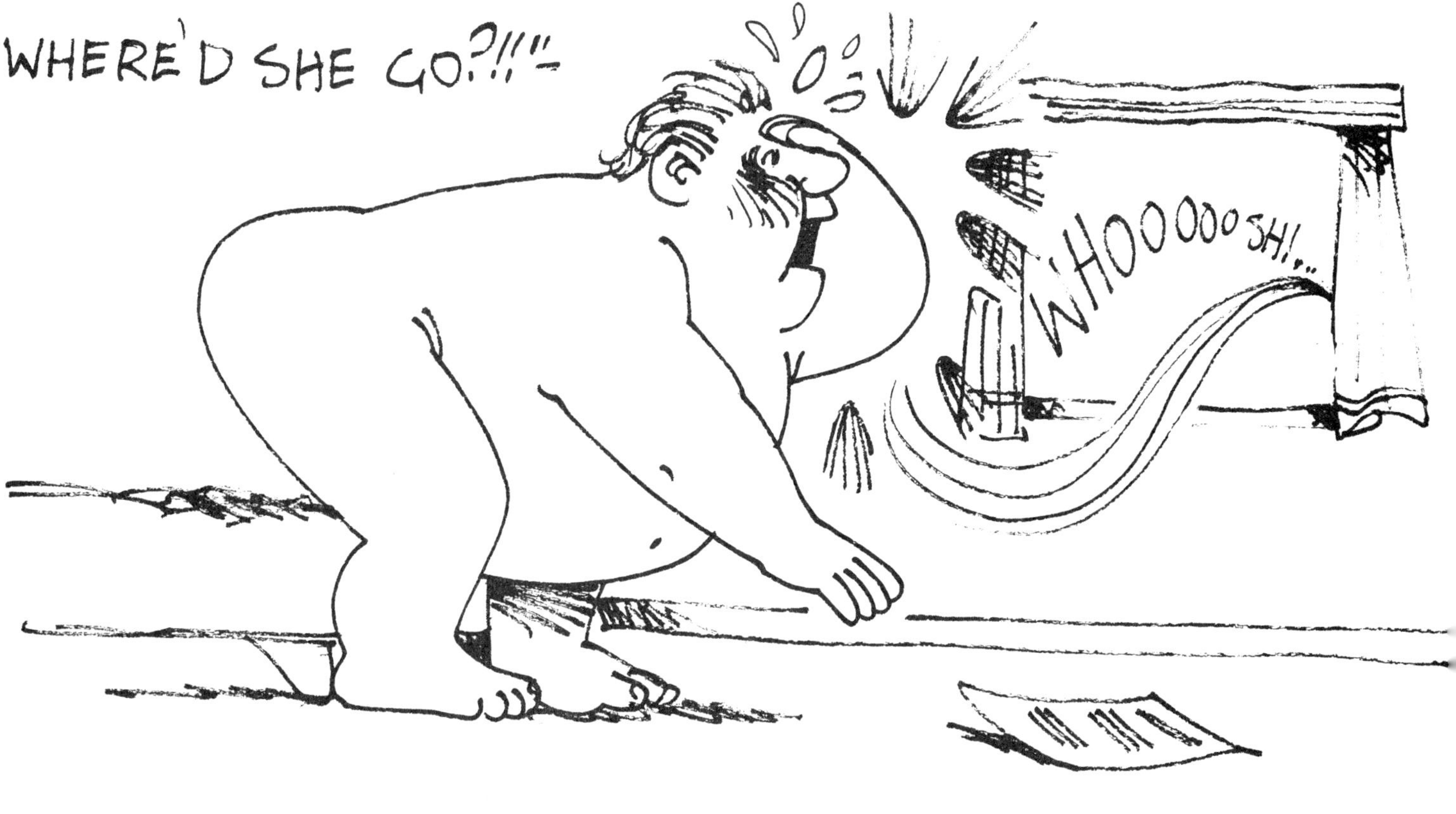

DON'T SMOKE DURING SEX WITH A BLOW-UP PARTNER...

AND DON'T HAVE PETS IN THE SAME ROOM.....

ELVIS, LEAVE THAT ALONE! THAT'S MINE!

WEIGHT LOSS WITH A BLOW-UP PARTNER CAN BE DISAPPOINTING...

—" THAT'S NOT FAIR, YOU'VE LOST MORE WEIGHT THAN I HAVE!"—

VIBRATORS:

GREAT FUN FOR SEX WITH ONESELF.

BUT AS A WEIGHT LOSS AID.

A DEAD LOSS...

ATMOSPHERE: PREPARING FOR YOUR PARTNER'S VISIT: ARE YOUR PETS GOING TO BE QUIET?

"DON'T LOOK SO SAD IT'S ONLY FOR THREE HOURS"

ONLY THREE HOURS!! WHAT ABOUT OUR EAR PLUGS

HAVE YOU TOLD YOUR MOTHER

YOU HAVE A FRIEND COMING FOR TEA?.....

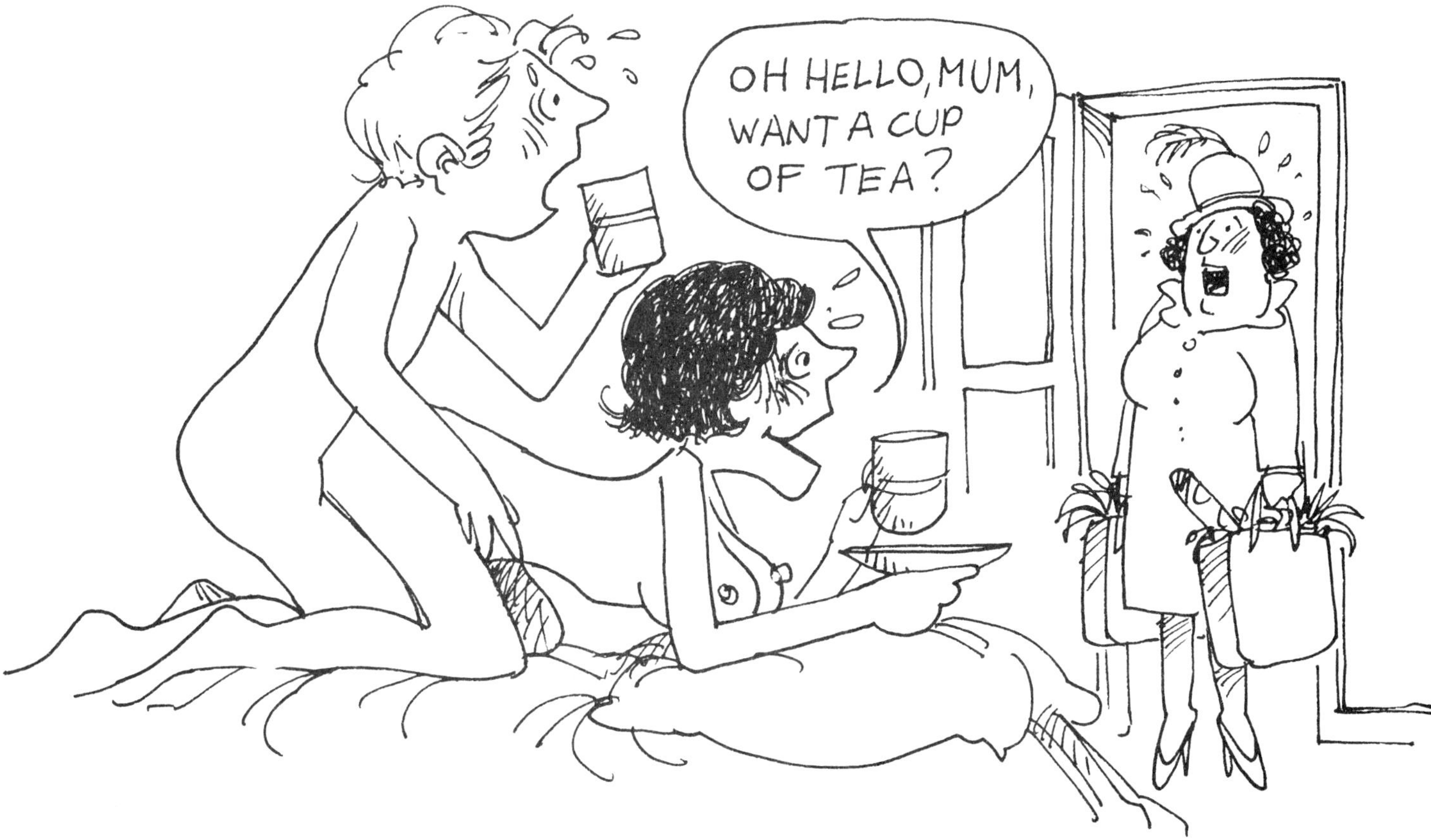

WHERE ARE THE CONDOMS?...

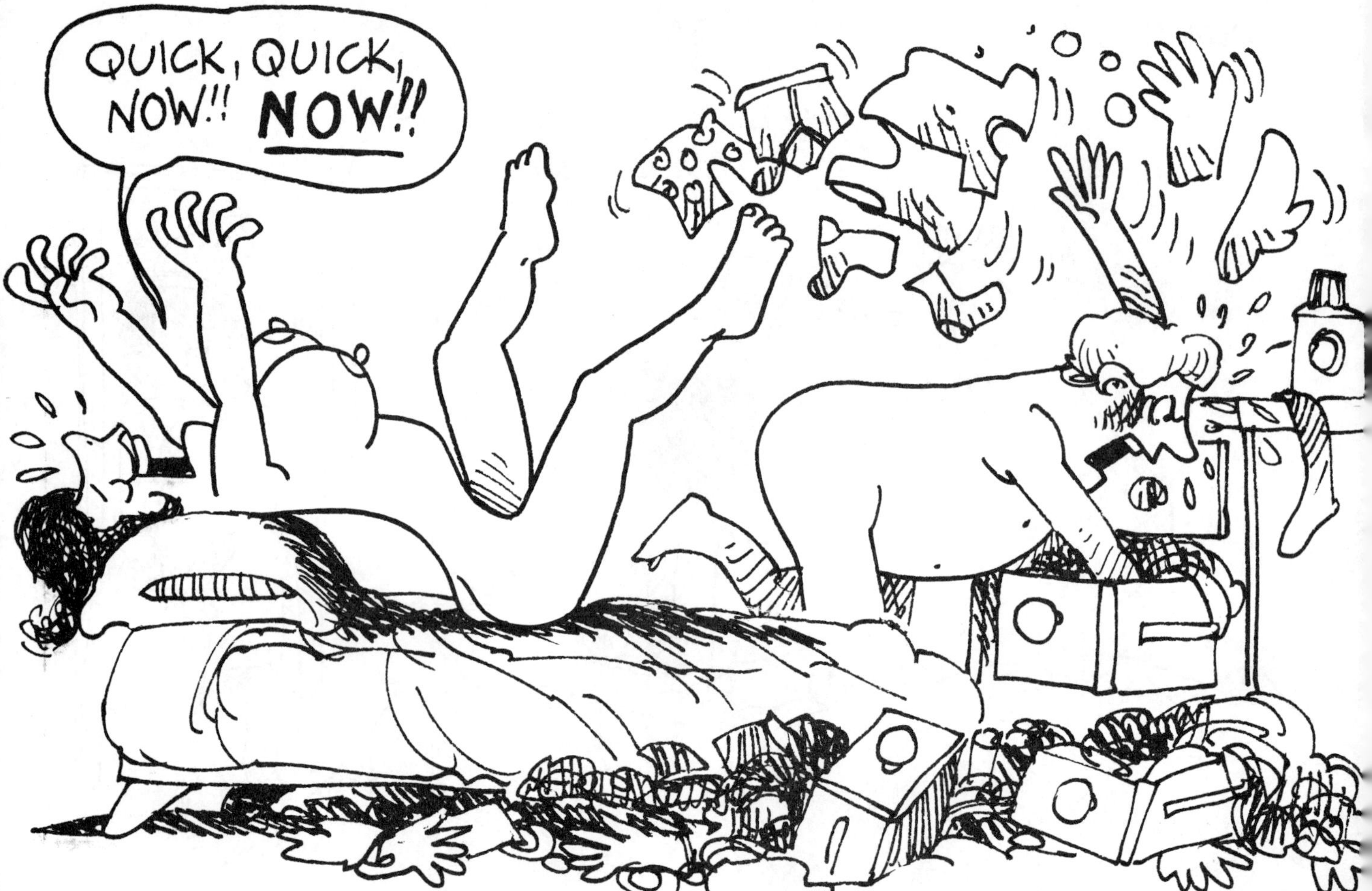

FOREPLAY:

THIS IS THE TIME WHEN ONE CAN LOSE MOST WEIGHT

- SO MAKE YOUR FOREPLAY <u>ACTIVE</u>!

"MISS JONES, THINK OF THIS, NOT AS SEXUAL HARRASMENT, BUT MORE OF A WEIGHT LOSING SITUATION...."

CHASING YOUR PARTNER AROUND THE BED CAN BE EXCITING.....
AND WEIGHT LOSS IS POSSIBLE...

MORE..

NOW INCREASE THE DRAMATIC SIDE OF THE CHASE -

......THIS CAN ENHANCE WEIGHT LOSS...

BLIND MAN'S BUFF...

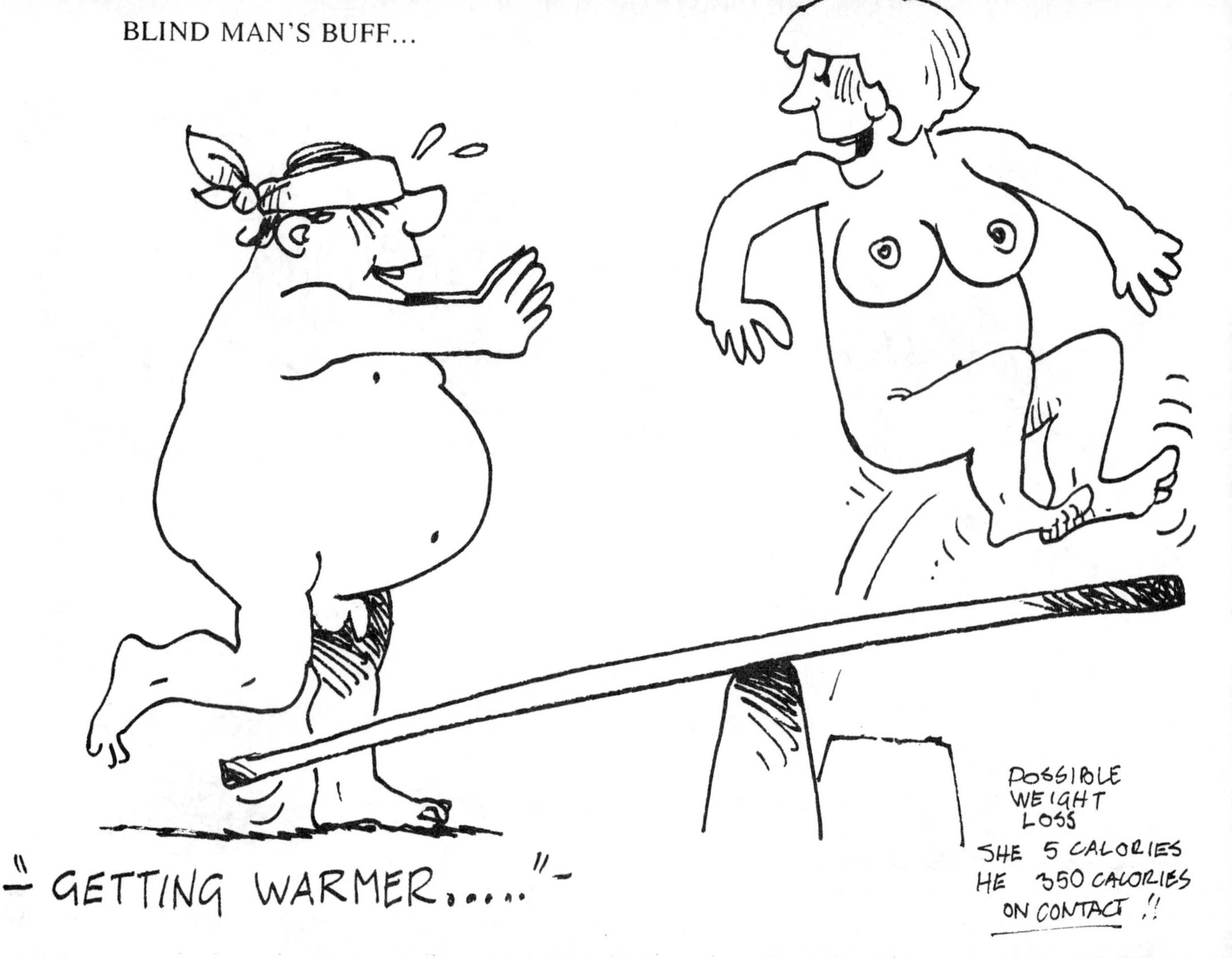

FOUR HOURS OF NAKED BONKING
- POSSIBLE WEIGHT LOSS: 23 CALORIES.

"THAT'S GREAT ARTHUR, ONLY 3 HOURS 58 MINUTES TO GO"

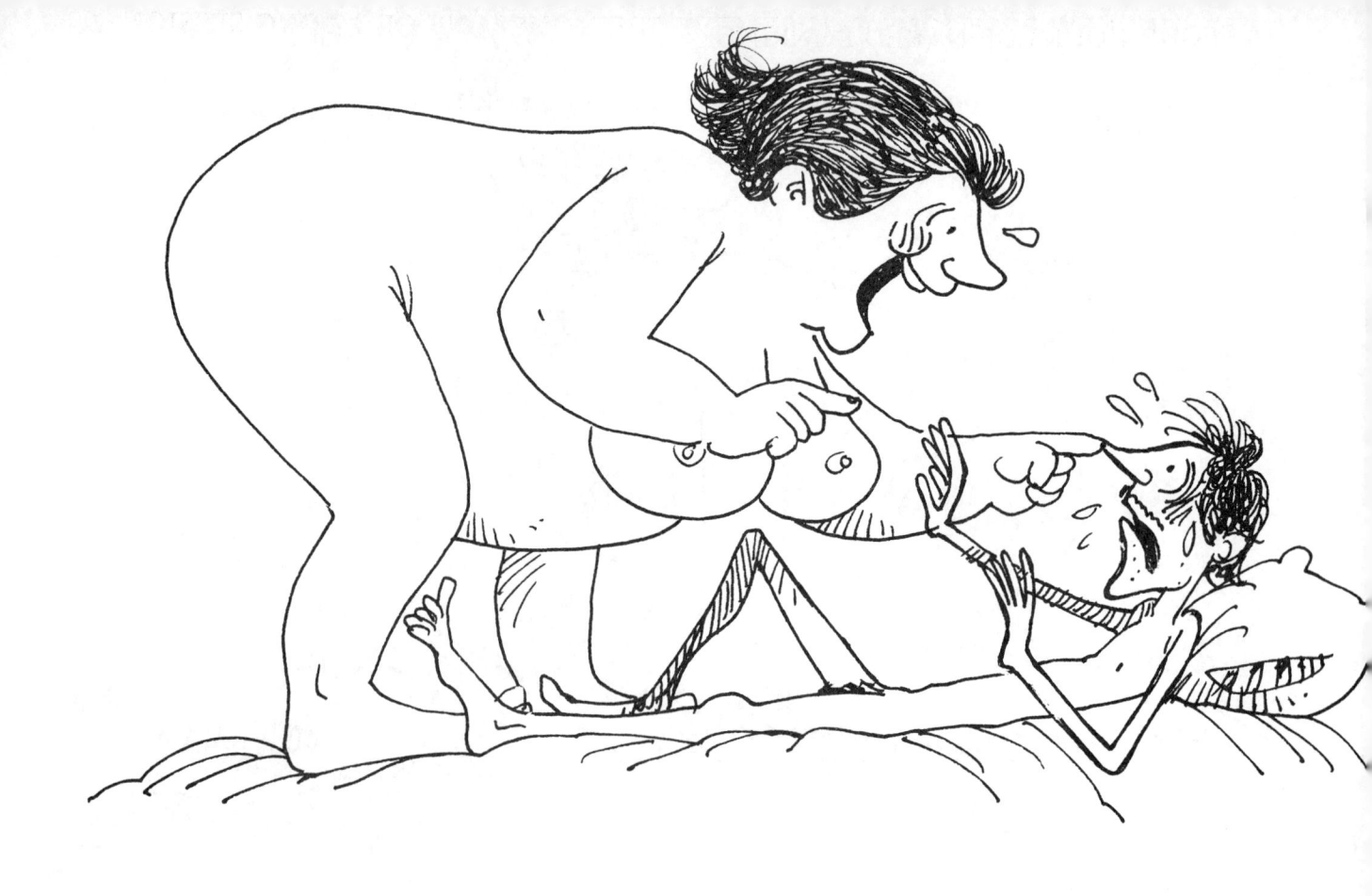

"READY TO HELP ME LOSE SOME MORE WEIGHT SWEETY PIE?"

TRYING NEW POSITIONS CAN RELIEVE THE MONOTONY OF A LONG SESSION...

"AND I SAY, WE CAN'T BOTH BE ON TOP!"-

TRY THE REVERSE POSITION...

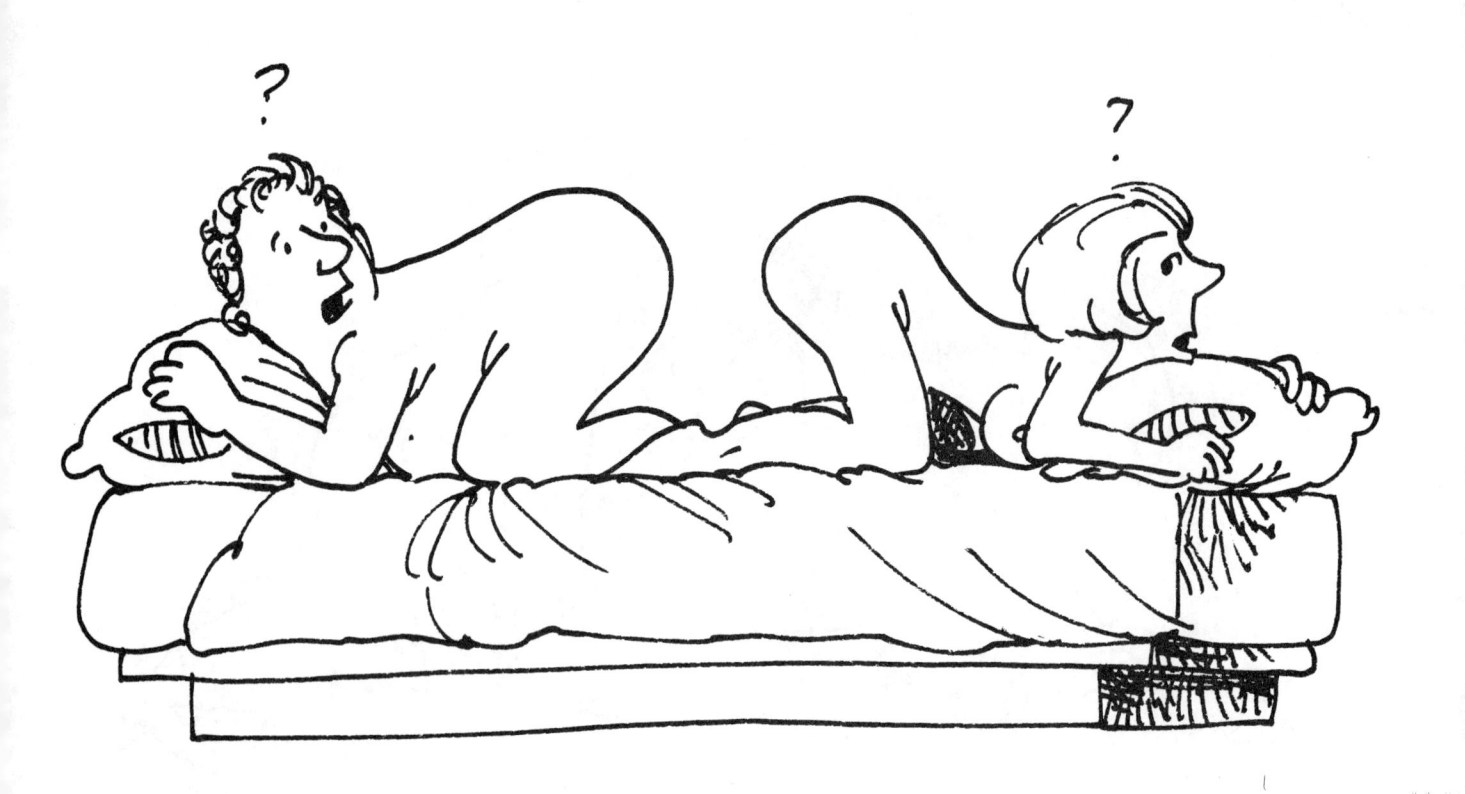

"WELL, NOW WHAT??"

TRY THE OTHER REVERSE POSITION...

—" WHAT DO I DO NOW? "—

SOME POSITIONS COULD BE DANGEROUS...

"GEORGE, WE'VE BURNT OFF 535 CALORIES, DO YOU WANT TO GO FOR THE 1000?"

"JUMP UP SWEETY AND WEIGH YOURSELF, LETS SEE HOW MUCH YOU'VE LOST....."

"WELL, IF I HAVEN'T LOST ANY WEIGHT, WE'RE GOING TO DO IT AGAIN, AND AGAIN TILL I DO!"

"TIME FOR SOME MORE HORIZONTAL JOGGING, DEAR"

DO YOU WANT TO TRY THE BANANA DIET AGAIN MARTHA?
BANANA? MORE LIKE A GERKIN IF YOU ASK ME...

"WHEN I SAID **YOU** SHOULD TRY THIS DIET, I MENT WITH **ANOTHER DOG**!!"

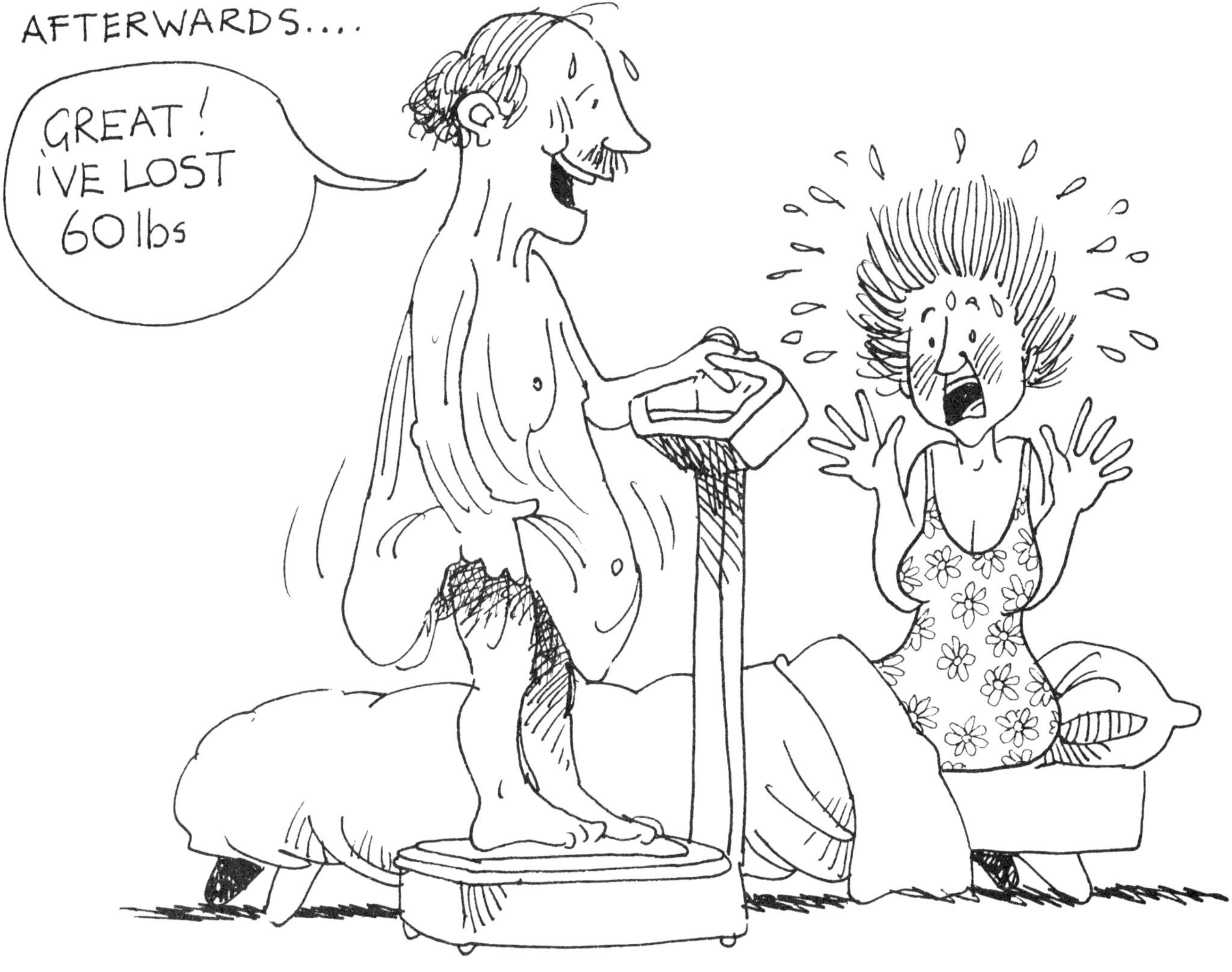
AFTERWARDS....
GREAT! I'VE LOST 60lbs

"CONGRATULATIONS! YOU'VE LOST THE MOST WEIGHT ON **THE NEW SEX DIET!!**"

..THANKS...

WE HOPE YOU'VE ENJOYED DOING **THE NEW SEX DIET!** AND LOST SOME WEIGH TOO!! AND IF YOU'VE TRIED EVERYTHING IN THIS BOOK AND YOU STILL HAVE'NT LOST WEIGHT, WELL, WHAT THE HECK, IT WAS FUN TRYING WASN'T IT??
WHY NOT TURN TO PAGE ONE AND START AGAIN.........

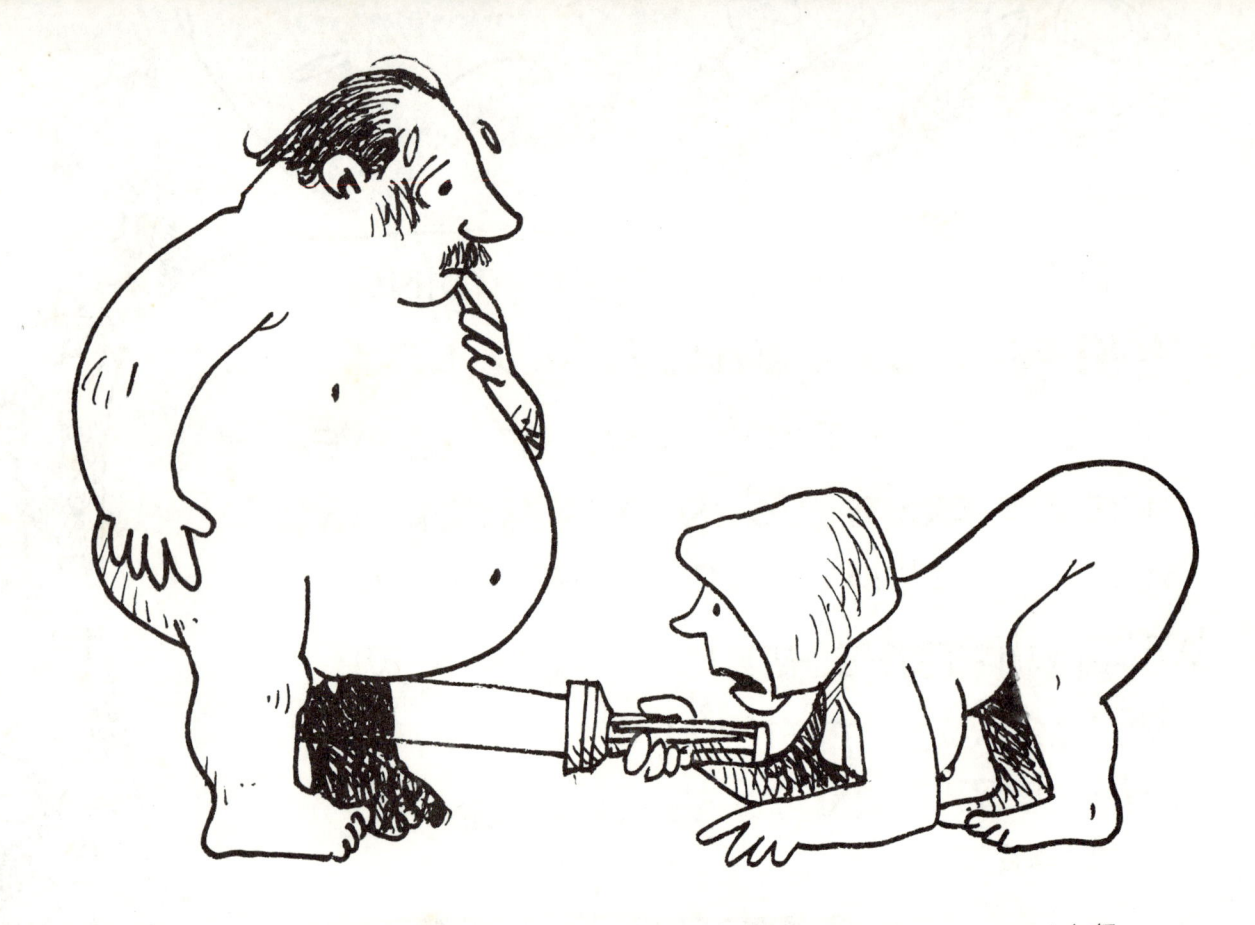

"WELL YOU'VE CERTAINLY LOST SOME WEIGHT THERE HAROLD."........